AFTER THIS WE GO DARK

Terri
thank you
for your
support

THERESA DAVIS

Theresa

Sibling Rivalry Press
Alexander, Arkansas
www.siblingrivalrypress.com

After This We Go Dark

Sibling Rivalry Press, LLC
13913 Magnolia Glen Drive
Alexander, AR 72002

www.siblingrivalrypress.com
info@siblingrivalrypress.com

ISBN: 978-1-937420-38-3

Library of Congress Control Number: 2013931745

First Sibling Rivalry Press Edition, May 2013

For my dad,

Charles "Jikki" Riley

Thank you for seeing me when I couldn't see myself

AFTER THIS

WE GO DARK

AFTER
THIS
WE GO
DARK

SATURDAY NIGHT LIVE

We often squatted there—the bed just a queen
but we all fit so it felt king-sized.
Family time in the room with the biggest television
happened nearly every Saturday night. Tonight,
Michael Jackson and Diana Ross will be singing to us.
It's a special night. We get to stay up late.

My sister worries a loose tooth. It is so loose that
it moves whenever she takes a breath. In and out—
it wiggles like a threat.

My brothers play checkers on the edge of the bed.
The younger brother lives for the triple jump.
"King me!" he yells, wanting everyone
to know of his victory. They've been playing
all day. He hasn't won a single game.
He wears hope like a Boy Scout badge.
His eyes are glazed. He will fall asleep
before the game is over.

The boyfriend soon-to-be-father begs
the younger daughter with the loose tooth
to let him pull it. She screams like she is on fire.
The older daughter reads *Tiger Beat*
while waiting for her future husband Michael
to smile at her from the glow of the television screen.
Soon she will be old enough to marry. He will see her
and fall in love. He will—as long as Diana is not around.

The older brother leaves the room. When he returns
he sees that the younger brother has fallen asleep,
his fingers wrapped around his king.

The younger daughter with the loose tooth has also
fallen asleep. The boyfriend soon-to-be-father
taps the older sister on the shoulder, places a finger
across his lips, points at the sleeping girl.

He pulls the tooth so easily, the girl never moves.
The older daughter, older brother, mom,
and boyfriend soon-to-be-father giggle
behind their hands.

Michael and Diana are singing now. The older daughter
has tears in her eyes. She wishes Diana would stop
touching her soon-to-be-one-day-husband.

The younger daughter stirs. She wakes. She staggers
to the bathroom. The toilet flushes.
She turns on the faucet to wash her hands,
looks in the mirror and notices
a change in her reflection. Grabs at her throat. Swears
she swallowed her tooth and now the Tooth Fairy
won't come. And she believes she is going to die.

At her cries the younger brother jerks awake,
fingers still clutched around the checkers.
He takes a triple jump, declares himself
the winner, falls back to sleep.

The boyfriend soon-to-be-father grabs up
the younger sister. Shows her the tooth. She smiles
a shaky smile. Thanks God she is not
going to die. She demands to be tucked into bed.
She doesn't want to piss off the Tooth Fairy
by making her wait.

The older boy puts the checkers in the box.
He puts the game away. He wakes
the younger brother. He will deposit him
on the lower bunk before he climbs onto the top.

The older daughter kisses Michael
goodnight. There are six posters of him
on the walls of her bedroom, his face at kissing level.
It will take some time. She settles in bed.
She sleeps with *Tiger Beat* under her pillow
while thoughts of Michael moonwalk in her head.

The mother and the boyfriend soon-to-be-father
tidy up. Ready themselves to do what grown folks do
in the dark. The house is quiet again.
Another Saturday night put to bed.

WORST CASE SCENARIO #1

What to do when you arrive at your home in the projects to find
high and drunken men shooting craps in front of your door

you are surprised
your octopus arms hold
one baby on hip
bag of groceries
the toddler by a hand
double stroller
you don't make direct eye contact
you remove the keys you need
hold them firmly between trembling fingers
you quietly say
excuse me
using only your head
you motion toward your door
when one man asks

bitch
what the fuck do you want

you do not tell him
instead you watch their bodies not their eyes
when one body relaxes you take a chance
look into that body's eyes
when he says

man
let this lady get by

you are grateful
reward him with full eye contact
you ignore the complaints from the other men
as they kind of
move away from your door
you juggle all the things you are holding
babies
stroller

groceries
your screams

you unlock the door quickly
not so quickly that they think you're afraid

you are afraid

when you feel the stroller
being pulled from your grasp
you tense
when you see it's the one
with the kind eyes you relax
but only a little
once inside
you engage all the deadbolts
you do this quietly
don't want them to think you are scared

you are terrified

you bathe the babies quickly
dress them in matching pajamas
sing lullabies
tell stories
when they are settled
you go to your front door
you peep though the peephole
watch
listen
as the game turns violent

you wear silent tears
check the locks on all the doors
all the windows
you go to your kitchen
remove a butcher knife from drawer
you go to your bedroom
you place the butcher knife under pillow
make a promise that you will

get your children out of the projects
you know that it won't be tonight
pray it will be soon

eventually
you cry yourself to sleep
hand gripping the handle of the blade

WORST CASE SCENARIO #2
What to do when you hear a woman being raped

you wake with a start
disoriented you stagger to your babies' room
when you find them sleeping soundly
you actually focus on what you are hearing

you go to your bedroom
remove butcher knife from under pillow
creep down the hallway to your back door
you peep through the peephole

you see the man
slap the woman
tell her to shut the fuck up
the calendar on the wall
tells you it is Sunday morning

you watch him tear at her clothing
he rips away her underwear
places his hand over her mouth
he begins his violation
and you hesitate
you want to save her
but you know that you can't
and you pray your babies can't hear

so
you call 9-1-1
whisper what you are hearing
you beg them
leave me anonymous
they say they will
you don't believe

you go to your kitchen window
peer through venetian blinds
you see the officer

one hand on holster
he talks into his shoulder
you hear a scream
run back to your backdoor
peep through the peephole
you see the man spit on the woman
pull up his pants and leave

you run back to your kitchen window
you see the officer
gun drawn
other hand held in a stop motion

you hear the man say
it was nothing
you see the woman stagger out
she screams she was raped
you see the officer
turn the man around
place handcuffs on his wrist
the officer looks up
he sees you
he nods
you panic
the ambulance comes
they all leave

you breathe
for what feels like the first time in days
you do the mom thing
make breakfast
talk baby talk
your head is a hamster wheel
you put your babies in their playpen
put on their favorite movie
it's *The Little Mermaid*

Ariel
she wants to be human
she wants to be a part of this world

and for some reason this is the saddest
thing you have ever heard
you are screaming in your chest
there is a knock on your front door
you tense then you peep
through the peephole
and you realize
you spend a lot of your life
peeping through peepholes

it's the officer from earlier
now in plain clothes
you are grateful
for the lack of uniform
you open the door
as much as the slide bolt will allow
he hands you a card
thanks you for calling in the assault
he tells you that all of your neighbors were home
all dressed to go to church and not one of them
thought about calling
he tells you that you are alone

you believe

he tells you if anything happens
call the number on the card
smiles when he hears your babies singing
you close the door
something inside of you breaks
your babies
they feel it
now everyone is crying
everyone
except for Ariel

Ariel
she sings

WORST CASE SCENARIO #3
What to do when opportunity knocks . . . or calls

you are standing over the phone
hands shaking nerves rattled
you are about to call your mother
beg her to let you come back home
with two children and all your shit

you are proud of your independence
but you know you are not safe here
you start to swallow your pride it hurts
the phone rings as your hand reaches for it
you jump
you notice you have become jumpy

you answer the phone
a woman's voice introduces herself
you know this woman
she asks if you are busy
you are not
she asks if you would come visit
she insists you bring the children
she knows you have no choice

you arrive sit in a classroom with ten children
you feel light for the first time in years
after you meet with this woman
with a smile she asks about your day
says she wants you to be their teacher
you laugh
she doesn't
you stop laughing
then you cry tell her about your week
about the drunken men about the rape
you tell her how unsafe you feel
she listens
you think you may have been hired
and fired within the same twenty minutes

when she asks what you need
you tell her you need to move
she walks to a drawer asks how much will it take
you don't know
she hands you a thousand dollars
tells you she'd like you to start the following week
and you don't move for a minute
you think about Ariel
you don't believe in fairy tales
so this must be something else

you move your life in two days
catch three buses and a train
to arrive at your new job
and when you get your first paycheck
you are prepared to sign it over to the woman
she asks what you are doing
you explain

she pretends she has no idea
what you are talking about
asks if your children need to eat
you say *yes*
do you need a winter coat
you say *yes*
she says you owe her nothing
you disagree
you owe her everything

you decide you will be good at this
because she said so

and you believe

SHELF LIFE

stoic sits on a shelf
staring aged ferocious
unfocused eyes
stills truth
steals time
tucked between teeth
bites down hard
on the word *sissy*
pray it fortifies his name

wipes away
punchline fists
sensitivity decorates
the floor splotches
sweeps under rugs
wayward domestic dogs
lap up what's left

he is angry

those starters of wars
hijack his safety
hallelujah tears have no place
on this landscape
no claim to his face
because his father
cannot smell pussy on his breath
insists on reminding him daily
he is no man

father's strong provider legs
take it out on his chest
burn away the fruitcake
baking under his mother's nurturing
he cannot afford to hold the softness of her

she does not understand

pretends not to see
that decency gets you gone
good posture
only puts your face
target level for blows
ass kicked in locker rooms
on street corners

father
cannot smell pussy on his breath
makes it his middle name
mother's baby boy
wrapped in soft sensitivity
he cannot live in the skin
she has wrapped him in
or survive
unless he is hard
so he will be hard
lock down emotion
place himself safely on a shelf
out of reach

SKIPPING STONES

fear is a stone in her chest
the weight so heavy she stands askew
her body a minefield
full of injured and broken places
step carefully or feel the shrapnel of her stare

she longs for quiet
so she may once again hear
the beating of her heart
longing for calm for peace

her surface is still
though her depths roil waves crash
do not drown
look her in the eyes
she will be surprised
may even return your stare

she speaks sometimes
says things like

no one lives their lives in the present
too caught up in the past
focused on an unseen future
be present in your life
so you do not forget who you ever were

I once saw her hands
dive deep into her pockets
she pulled out a handful of stones
looked at them like they were secrets
she placed one in her smiling mouth
the others back in their pocket home

she looked lighter then
her steps so lively
she was almost skipping

CONVERSATIONS
for Dr. Lorraine Wilson

I have been speaking with the dead
removed from my physical proximity
but rattling through my lungs like oxygen
regimented pain
reminding me of purpose
as I hurl myself unflinching
unblinking in the glow
of luminescent tomorrows
without you

I have been speaking with the dead
to she who is reluctant to reveal
my amputated dreams
but keeps me in her good graces

and because I love her
I have to tell her

there are those who would defame you
sprinkling disreputable memories
in the well waters of your goodness
those discontents roaming aimlessly
shattering voices unheard

she speaks to me in dreams
her melancholic whispers
prevent my fevered reconsideration
she knows she showed me my future
became my past in what seemed like the same breath

in my remembrance I explode backwards
my rarely punctuated heartbeat runs on
sentencing me daily to begin again without her
but those lingering pomegranate sunsets
ready me for her meticulous inspection
we see the same stars

I will continue building this legacy we started together
grateful that she armed me with conviction
and my condemnation will not falter in her absence
I will illuminate every horizon revealed to me

because

I am not angry any more
my insomniatic refusals
to continue conversations
we started when she was in the flesh
no longer call for my rancor

though there are days when her presence
is skin I have never shed
there are days when the rustling of leaves
resembles her laughter and I spin on my heels
seeking her face in the barks of dead trees

there are days when I miss her
like teeth

but I promise I am not angry any more
I know she would have given her life to be here
and I am here eagerly awaiting the blanket
of stars she will cover me with
so that when slumber finally takes me
she and I
we will continue this conversation

SATURDAY

Saturdays have always been my favorite day of the week
not for the sleeping-in factor but because of my childhood
my parents had us trained
mom and dad
not bio dad but the dad that stuck around

because if on Saturday
we were awakened by the smell
of oatmeal drenched in brown sugar
and Elton John screaming through
the speakers that the bitch was back
we knew it was a cleaning day

but if on Saturday
we were awakened by the smell
of pancakes bacon and eggs
we could finish breakfast find ourselves
at a museum or a protest rally

but every once in a Saturday
we were awakened by a phrase
post office day
we would dress ourselves quickly
Garanimal ensured we were not tacky
lion with lion giraffe with giraffe

we would inhale our cold cereal breakfast
and prepare ourselves for the walk to the post office
halfway there was a Velvet Freeze
if we were good we'd have ice cream

we all had jobs at the post office
I would stand at the interior post office door
warn my mother of oncoming post office employees
my brother was the official licker of the stamps
and I am convinced that he is the reason
stamps now are adhesive

my younger siblings were handed
fists full of change and instructed to feed
the lemonhead machine
my mother would then lazily languidly
rifle through pamphlets and flyers
inevitably ending at a three-ringed binder
attached to the wall by a hook

when she returned the book
our jobs were done
me by her side
my brother handing her envelopes
stamps sliding off their sides
my younger siblings would give us each
a sweaty palmful of lemonheads
my mother would slip something in her pocket

as we approached the Velvet Freeze
we were on our best behavior
and once I had a meeting with my siblings
where I explained that if we ordered Neapolitan ice cream
it would be like having three scoops instead of one

Saturday
post office day

my dad he passed away on a Saturday
his memorial service held on a Saturday
and to this day I still have people commenting
that that was the best memorial service
they'd ever been to guiltily stopping themselves
before they ask
so when's the next one

we were a mess when he left
our atoms bumping into each other
threatening to rearrange themselves

going through his things
I came across a folder inside paper all the same

28

three rings ripped out of the top like band-aids

I read one

Wanted by the FBI, Charles Riley Jr.

there are ten fingerprints
three photos
one in profile
one head on
and one where he looks so smooth
they way I remember him

*Riley, Black Panther, is wanted for teaching the building and
use of incendiary devices knowing how those devices would be
used. Riley has been known to carry a handgun or rifle.
Consider him armed and dangerous.*

my heart tells me my mother took them
because he was ours
and if one less person recognized him
that would give us one more day
and the ice cream was a celebration
of that one more day
I laugh then cry tears of remembrance
and my love of Saturday

every once in a while I find myself
in the post office and if I happen across one
antiquated enough to have that book I flip through it
and when I don't see his picture I smile
then curse gentrification because
there are no longer ice cream parlors
every eight blocks

now I think I want three scoops
chocolate
vanilla
and strawberry
because as long as I have Saturday

I have love
family
sliding stamps
sweaty palms full of lemonheads
my mom
feeling light
and memories of you

Charles Riley Jr.
my dad
for one more day

VENTRILOQUIST

fingers slide up down her xylophone spine
tapping out the sad soliloquy of unfinished
tickling stroking pulling thin strings
holding self-esteem between strong fingers
a simple flick of the wrist
a simple phone call
he will break the spell
break her as well

poised on his knee she sits lifeless
until he works his magic
her tongue connected to levers
mimic his sound
if she does not behave
if she says the wrong thing
he will cover her mouth

she turns her head only when he turns it
opens her eyes only if he removes the blinders
obedient pupil she learns well knows early
he will discard her like the other toys
that looked like her
bodies bent to fit a mold
wrapped in lies that provide no warmth

they themselves removed
thrown away
coffeehouse bar flies stuck in a verbal time warp
believing through their disbelief in tarnished gold
obedient puppet only moving when directed
only speaking when spoken through
and his lips
they never move

ROUGH SEAS TWISTED LOVE

we have no business being together

we roam in search of plunder
unrecognizable to our eyes
heedful of consequences
marked by the absence of good luck
you my love are no heads-up penny
you lack delicacy sensitivity and character
but the taste of your copper in my mouth intrigues

my reverie interrupted by the cadence of your speech
which lacks sense reason and judgment
you get by because of my overabundant supply
of platitudes and acquiescence
I allow you to manipulate me
sickly attracted to your archipelago heart

we are love's renegades
marauding pillaging our way through
and around each other our tarnished souls in rhythm
refusing to conform leaving no room for interpretation
we control our fortunes choose to treasure
our time despite our bellicose tantrums of the contrary

we have no business being together

when you are gone I do not miss you
you enter my thought as after
when the lashes scab over
my flesh no longer tingles at the mention of your name
I set sail for smoother seas for calm and normal
realizing I am neither
the ache surfaces
no amount of circumnavigation can get around
my need to be once again caught in your undertow

drag me under
sink your teeth in my flesh
I am no fan of upheaval
but accepting of all that is familiar indulgent
assuage myself on the sweetness of you
we form move in waves
this ship rocks in celebration of your coming

you are a wayward projectile
I am X-marks-the-spot
crashing on your shore
you my siren song
my renegade lover
manipulating marauder
pillager of my peace

we have no business being together

OVER EASY

it would be easy to resist the urge to wake
close my eyes go back to sleep
dream myself the definition of normal
the epitome of conformity
ignore the rattle of bones
muse them wind chimes
let that safety envelop me
let fear obscure my vision
because maybe if I don't see myself clearly
neither will you

I wonder if I could ever live like you
so I could avoid
the suspension bridge of doubt
that has me swaying to the beat of different drums
staple my tongue to my teeth never utter a word
so I don't resemble my broken lines
get lost in the margins
allow the narrow-minded views
of equally narrow-minded people
to measure me believe the lie
that true peace is elusive

shy away from that need
to bear naked again
as I drift away from me
like a ghost in the midst of a haunting
living life cautiously content
peering through the slither view of key holes

it would never work

I don't care for confined spaces
and closets make me look invisible
don't afford me my panoramic views
I don't do too many things easy
I tend to scream like the noise will protect me

because the noise will protect me
and normal is fucking boring

when my skin craves her touch
like the wings of birds crave air
I'm touching and flying
feel free not to watch
conformity confines
and I will be damned
if I let your underlying hate
paint me anything other than human
so judge me if you want
because this is all you are going to get

FAITHFULLY

perfectly willing to rely on faith
I offered my heart
scripted in the lines of this poem
it lives in my pocket
so I can remember it all
I constantly re-read it to
diminish your reflection
douse the flames erupting
when your eyes fix me

your eyes

once lovely and inviting
now hollow points
empty but deadly
constantly watching
judging my movements
this dance that lacks rhythm
leaves me dizzy
seeking the truth in your blank stare
I am afraid to blink
in fear of becoming a target
lined up in your sight
the bull's eye painted on my exposed heart
and foolish me

I eagerly await your impact
the pain worth your pleasure
you love me like a natural disaster
leaving nothing in your wake
except my devotion
a love manifest
that has labeled me broken
and I do
I understand your tempestuous nature
but if it's true that murderers come back
as the ones they have killed

one day you'll wear my face
this poem in your pocket
the remnants of my heart
clinched between your teeth

faithfully

DUST

and after the explosion the dust settles
we don't look like ourselves
but we look the same
weep concrete tears
that carve paths down cheeks
but offer no redemption
so we shield our faces
ignore truth's dagger stare

we explode often
throwing tantrums beneath bed sheets
then wipe the grit of regret from our eyes
because like the dust
we've settled

I remember
when I first found the depth in your gaze
when I drowned in your smile
we embraced the wild torrents of our affection
caught our breath on the other side of release
sometimes we just held onto each other
our bodies merging creating a synergy
that balanced the cosmos
kept the constellations in place
we never held our tongues
we spoke of love with our whole mouths

but lately
the face I used to read so well
has rendered me illiterate
you speak in a tongue I do not recognize
my name drips from your lips napalm
we explode from lack of concession
I mean who wants to be wrong
when this love feels so right

your hugs are punches
my mouth touching yours
is a kin to French kissing electric sockets
we singe both too strong to yield we crumble
become accustomed to the numbness
ignore the ache in our hearts
until the anger seizes
then we touch

fingernails on chalkboards
tainted
foreign to the passion we once shared
this is fucking frightening
but at least it's contact
we tear at our seams
willing them to break
so we can fall away from each other
before we crumble

and after the explosion the dust settles
we don't look like ourselves
we look the same
weep concrete tears
that form paths down cheeks
but offer no redemption
so we shield our faces
wipe the grit of regret from our eyes
because like the dust
we've settled

I'M READY

I'm ready

not like last time
when ready was laced with limitations
scattered with the same dust
as memories and broken promises

once upon a time
she played love on my heart strings
a complicated melodic notion of the future
lyrics stuffed into the mouth of this girl
with apocalyptic fantasies of forever
pipe dreams that left stigmata across my chest
forced whispers forced me into locked closets
suffocated by relentless stares
that bounced off of my skeptical smile and rebounded
let's call that a trick of the moonlight

time has this way of mending memories
with embellishments
that make past tense, future perfect love possible
turns unimaginable torture
hell and damnation
into an earthly paradise
because even now
wings of beauty unfurl in my belly

every time I think of her
sweet voiced
she spoke eloquently
the most exquisite of earthbound angels
and I was anointed
I was immaculate
I lacked nothing
except faith
since the day I fell from grace
I've been plagued by taciturn

expressions previously deemed volcanic
necessities of self-preservation
I have never let my guard down since then
my misplaced energy turned miserable into miseries
and failure that filled long long loveless nights
and I never let my eyes linger too long for fear of
sparking sensations

but now I am tired of hibernation
tired of mending heart stings
canonized by her departure
when the thought of losing myself inside another
was more frightening than losing me

but now
I'm ready

open me up
lace my disjointed dreams
around your fingers
baby pull them apart
weave me white light and scattered molecules
allow every color of this rainbow to show
and don't you dare
belie my madness
see me for who I am
skewed logic and halcyon sunsets
color me golden hues of the rest of my life
emancipated from closed-off expectations
trace my rhythmically challenged
heartbeat back to before

proselytize me
preempt my defense mechanisms
girl rise and fall with me
make me believe in love again
come on

I'm ready

BREATHING LESSONS

I never heard the term *LUG*
lesbian until graduation
before my thirties
so I never knew in my college days that
that's what they were calling me
behind suppressed giggles and raised eyebrows
all I knew then
was that she was beautiful

the first time our eyes met
she took my breath away
I didn't know why I would find myself
where she was
stumbling across her path
avoiding eye contact
but always
always found staring

the day she called me by name
my knees buckled visibly
she caught me by the arm
grinned me a disarming grin
and whispered in my ear
if you breathe you won't pass out

her words buzzed through me like electricity
and for a week after that whenever our eyes met
there was a mad blush and an intake of breath
I could not release

she would sometimes scream across a room

BREATHE

people thought she was crazy
but I thought proudly
yeah she's talking to me

the day she asked me out after a game
she the baller and me believe it or not
holding pom-poms
I accepted greedily
without thinking about this thing
I couldn't stop thinking about
clueless to my surroundings
the tittering whispers the jeers
hell I figured if they wanted me to hear them
they'd speak up
because I was much too busy trying to master
this whole breathing thing
I didn't understand the pull she had on me
and at no time did it seem problematic

I once described the feelings to my mother
draped in a lie where
she became Lee and I was my friend
my mother's only comment

that sounds like love

the first time she kissed me
I think I left my body
when I returned she lay over me
stroking my cheek reminding me

baby breathe

I never told her I loved her
I freaked out when I heard
my name and *gay* in the same sentence
it never occurred to me
that a word used so frequently to diminish
shrouded in hate laced with harsh tones
could be used to describe what I shared with her

she once told me boldly
confidently that she loved me
she wanted to know if I loved her too

and in tears I lied

no
loving you would be
problematic

painfully I watched her dissolve
and when she stormed from the room
she took the air with her
and I forgot
to breathe

when I awoke
not on the floor where I fell
but placed lovingly on the bed
where we shared our secret
she lay over me
a cool towel pressed to my head
a resuscitating kiss pressed to my lips
she reminded me again

baby you've got to remember
you've got to breathe

and I watched her
gather her things
preparing to walk out of my life
she gave me one last kiss that left me cold
and parting words that burned
loving you was never problematic for me

part of me wants to find her
now that I'm an adult and I know who I am
and I want to tell her that whole breathing thing
has never been a problem since she left
because no one has ever
completely taken my breath away
the way she did

part of me wants to go back in time
to the exact moment that lie fell from my lips
I want to take it back
tell her what my heart now knows

and all of me wants to thank her
for being my first possibly my only true love
I want to let her know

baby I've been practicing

and if I ever fall in love like that again
thanks to you
I will
I will remember

and I'll breathe

BECAUSE SHE THINKS SHE IS GOING TO HELL

honey

you are not being judged
because your bones decided
maybe in a moment unplanned
to rest near my bones

passion has no punishment
except the ones
we place upon our own hearts

I mean
we were runaway trains that night
and I was wearing my voice
at just the right decibel

you never stood a chance

besides
I understand those urges
that make you question things
like sexuality and I want to know
what this feels like
regret doesn't live in my heart
it simply can't afford the rent
and I am no test dummy
no one takes advantage of me
without my permission
if your tongue is tied
my prayer is that your thoughts are not
I am drawn to all things beautiful
and like it or not you were
you are beautiful

I mean
we were a head-on collision that night
and I never saw you coming
well
until I did

HANDS

it starts with a touch
one that excites and aggravates
smooth lines on parchment
searching for secrets
tucked between folds
my name in your mouth a breath held
spoken into the locks that circle my head
a crown
I am a queen here
locked in your embrace
hold me to the light
watch me shine sparkle
moans like music we dance
slow at first
our momentum increases
your eyes glass
we slide shimmer
my mouth turns filthy
the words all guttural stain
I don't believe my own ears
you ask me what I want
Pandora's box opens
just enough to let simple sins flow
out in tangles of sheets and palms
we become elastic
stretching more than intentions
bend like willows roll like waves
crash and break holding like notes
we are an opera
we are a memory in the making
shaking leaves falling forever
it started with a touch

PICKLES AND PEPPERMINTS
for Dennis

the first boy who kissed me received a punch in the chest
but I let him sit next to me in the lunchroom
let him share my Oreos (not the cream)
I wasn't that easy then

the first boy who kissed me received a punch in the chest
soon learned to move quickly in and out of coat rooms
he left notes in my pockets
daily reassurances
I always checked *yes*

the first boy who kissed me received a punch in the chest
then complained that I never let him catch me when playing tag
suggested I run slower
act like a girl
I whirled on him
he spit dirt for ten minutes

the first boy who kissed me received a punch in the chest
became jealous when I got picked before him at dodgeball
told the other boys to stay away from me
told them I belonged to him
I showed him my fist
asserted my freedom
then helped him wash the blood from his shirt

the first boy who kissed me received a punch in the chest
left a Valentine on my desk one February
right next to a bagged pickle and a peppermint
the other girls only got chocolate
it felt like love

the first boy who kissed me received a punch in the chest
then one weekend went fishing with his father
there was a problem with the boat
bodies fell into the water
and the first boy who kissed me
forgot to float

KEYS

I don't lock my car
I have not locked it in years
not in my neighborhood
I have learned instead to leave nothing of value inside
and if it is stolen maybe it will be returned
but if the windows are busted out that deductible
will be a motherfucker
so I don't lock my car

I have a neighbor she disappeared for a while
has absence was noticed
months later she reappeared
her children grandchildren in tow
I thought this will make her happy
how many times have I heard glow about her babies
my wave and smile are ignored
she looks at me
as if she has not looked at me these now five years
her daughter's smile wears hinges
later she will tell me of Alzheimer's and locked doors

my neighbor is standing in her front yard
it is two o'clock in the morning
I know this because I cannot sleep
the words marching through my thoughts angry ants
I am also in my front yard
she taps at her pockets moves from car to car

my car is unlocked
I haven't locked it in years
my porch a stage away from the lights
I grab at the keys on my hip
I click at the remote
the horn sounds
she looks aloft
possibly seeking Gabriel in our southern skies
a light comes on in her home

her daughter now in the yard coaxes cajoles
promises her a ride in the car tomorrow

and I fear she is tossing lies on the bonfires
that are her mother's memories

at first
I don't understand the tears
racing suicide down my face toward pavement
I throw my head back an effort to reclaim them
see Orion standing in his darkness
belt winking

so
I offer up a prayer to the night
pray my neighbor dreams
convertible of wind blowing through her hair
head bobbing to the music only she can hear
keys jangling in the ignition
as she races toward her memories
and just
drives

SMOKE AND MIRRORS

While her sisters were immortal, Medusa was not

Why am I still here?

I only wanted to see the sun.
Feel it kiss my skin, caress my face.
I had spent so much time being cold,
an existence not meant for me not here.
Not now. Not ever. I am daughter of earth,
of the ocean. And yes, Poseidon was attracted
to the scent of salt on my skin.
I did not lure, I did not plot,
I did none of those things.
That kind of woman, I have never been.

Seems Athena confused me with her fickle self.
She who is prone to trickery and disguise.
Poseidon raped, pursued me.
And yes, he lapped unwelcome at my shores,
and for that she would deny me the sun?

By asking I was merely being polite.
I shouldn't have had to ask.
Her denial spoke of the jealousy I accused,
brought the truth to the light she tried to deny me.

So she can have my beauty. Turn me freak.
Make me monster. I was born of the earth,
the ocean, a tribal warrior woman.
She should have know that women
move me more than men
ever could.

Hell, it almost seems appropriate
they turn stone cold under my gaze.
As long as they know that is the gift she gave
to them. And despite her cruelty,
despite her mangled sense of propriety, I have won!

The sun has seen my face,
a sight she will never forget.

And the snakes . . . the snakes keep my countenance.
Their constant hissing reminds me that my strength
resides within. Have you seen the way I lift up women
brave enough to own my stare?

She actually did me a favor, that Athena.
Showed the world how ugly she really was
by making me more resilient than she will ever be.

Why am I still here?

I am here to remind true Medusa women
their strength, their beauty, their power
resides within.

Regardless of what men or mirrors see.

STATE OF BEING

you be woman
nine months pregnant
full of hope and apprehension
he be deadbeat dad of the future
but you
you be hopeful
knowing you can do this by yourself
wondering if you can do this by yourself
you be working and surviving
making house into a home
preparing for who's to come
you be scared
sometimes
but pushing forward
you
you be in labor
pushing more than dreams
and he
after eighteen hours of devotion
he crowns and
he be perfect
you count his toes and fingers
just to be sure
his tearful cries announce his arrival
you be exhausted but proud
too many emotions to pinpoint one
he grips your finger
you be amazed at his strength
imagine it mirrors you own
your smile expands wider
than gravity should allow
despite the shake in your arms
you hold him close
his baby smell assaults your senses
you
you be in love
he be you

you be he
you put your face right on top of his
whisper a prayer wrapped in a promise
he opens his beautiful one-day brown eyes
accepting all that is life
all that is you together
you stare into the eyes of your future
your future stares back
you relax your jaw
unclench your spine
unhinge your apprehension
close your eyes
not to sleep
but to marvel
you understand
that now
you be mother
he be son
and all
be right in the world

FOR THE LADY

You look so tired, so used up. Maybe you should step, sit down.
Forever poised in the act of stepping away from the chains that
once held you. Your arms full of lies as you beckon those you now
wish to send away. You weren't built a liar from another land.
You acquired it like debt.

Forever poised in the act of stepping away from the chains that
once held you. Walking toward the abstract of freedom, an idea
with back doors. You weren't built a liar from another land. You
acquired it like debt. You've become a symbol without true
meaning and you cannot shield your eyes.

Walking toward the abstract of freedom, an idea with back doors.
Nothing here was ever free. The cost of your restoration proved
that. You've become a symbol without true meaning and you
cannot shield your eyes. You say nothing. Have you too adopted
the stance of don't ask, don't tell?

Nothing here was ever free. The cost of your restoration proved
that. If the words on your pedestal are removed, will you fall? You
say nothing. Have you too adopted the stance of don't ask, don't
tell? Was your immigration a choice or, like millions of slaves,
were you forced?

If the words on your pedestal are removed, will you fall? Are
Emma's words strong enough to keep you aloft? Was your
immigration a choice or, like millions of slaves, were you forced?
With your torchlight do you still seek the poor, the tired, or is it a
warning?

Are Emma's words strong enough to keep you aloft? Can you feel
the meaning of those words through the soles of you feet? With
your torchlight do you still seek the poor, the tired, or is it a

warning? *Stay away. The former slave owners have returned. Save yourself!*

Can you feel the meaning of those words through the soles of you feet? You have become the gift most unappreciated. *Stay away. The former slave owners have returned. Save yourself!* You look so tired, so used up. Maybe you should step, sit down.

451

Ignition temperature is the temperature
at which something catches fire
and burns on its own

4

those who fan the flames of ignorance
growing something larger than fear
they grow hate hang it around their words
disguise the truth they call it religion
they call it terror they call it patriotism
the written word has always been incendiary
full of hope and heart such bullshit in modern times
because now we the people we know better
we know how to hold the match steady
balance it on the tips of forked tongues
and throw it round like democracy
like assumptions
like global insight a riot
like church and state
so fan the flames media moguls

my God is bigger than yours

5

pillars of faith affirmation
prayer alms fasting pilgrimage
peace and protection
divine intervention
speaking in tongues
the father the son and the spirit
holy ghosts of past transgressions future redemption
this wine is my blood this bread is my body
all outstretched arms and right angles
eyes turned toward heaven sacraments
make me clean make me holy
and Florian patron saint of firefighters
bless us keep the flames from spreading

1
nation under God indivisible
with liberty and justice for all
lyrics spoon fed by false idols who never
intended for us to learn the art of
self-interpretation because that idea of tolerance
it ignites so hot it could burn down global communities
tiblioclast this is libricide and please remember
that the Nazis burned more than books
oh emulator
I never thought you'd show your face here
but hooded or not I'd recognize those eyes anywhere

451 degrees Fahrenheit
the temperature
at which book paper catches fire and burns
so you can disagree with the words
written on pages held together with a spine
tucked between covers filled with peace
joy love and terror
but fire unlike you it doesn't discriminate
our frail flesh and bone bodies
we're all different like ideals
this bone our sinew
we all have different ignition temperatures
different sparks that will set us aflame
but fire
fire knows exactly what temperature
it needs to reach to burn a book
and could give a goddamn
whether you have read the words

or not

FOR THE WOMEN OF THE CONGO

Now that you have touched the
women you have struck a rock,
you have dislodged a boulder,
you will be crushed.

Women's Freedom Song, August 1956

continental shifts only change our geography
the topography of pain still prevalent
concrete or dirt
our feet walk the same paths
streaked in blood
sweat
trials
tribulations
fingers tangled
screams swallowed
womb traitors
your fear betrays you

violence
your cowards way out

and still
we wipe constellations from our eyes
rest hands on hips that bear the world's pain and sorrow
women know
what the future looks like
umbilical cords of hope tie us to our oppressors
we know
that without us you would not be here
to spread your violence
full circle
to we
who are
your grandmothers
your mothers
your sisters
your daughters

your fear betrays you
rape our flesh
rape your homeland
starve your futures
you have forgotten where you come from
sold your souls to neglect
noosed your necks with torn hymens
that stretch the globe
marking times past and present
nothing is forgotten here
women are no foreigner to pain
nurture in our nature
you mistake it for weakness
you murders
of motherhood
of humanity
we nurtured you in our womb
cradled you to our breast
let life touch the back of your throat
and like levees we break
sometimes
but make no mistake about this

> *Now that you have touched the*
> *women you have struck a rock,*
> *you have dislodged a boulder,*
> *you will be crushed.*

and the warm flowing womb waters
that once embraced you
will no longer tolerate these transgressions
and we will no longer birth you by water
womb traitors
it will be by fire

next time

DIVINITY FOR DUMMIES

Pat Robertson said the 2010 Haiti earthquake was God's punishmer
for Haitian slaves' pact with the devil to win freedom from France

even if the angels were listening
even if the God you claim to represent
endorsed you plastered a swoosh on your smarmy soul
even if mother nature acknowledges your particular form of hate
wraps her tsunami legs around your waist and tremors
you until your voice registers richter
the ancestors know what you really want to say

so
loosen your tongue Pat
let your words laced in stupidity and self-righteousness
flow from you like the river Styx
your hateful undertones are nothing new
and if you believe in a God
who sanctions the ownership of bodies
while you preach freeing of the spirit the soul
then let your jackal tongue flap
let rhetoric hang on your every word
hypocrisy has nested well within you Pat
and the bees refuse to pollinate in such a place
so there will be no honey for the milk of human kindness
that sours on the tip of your tongue
the way you prey on those who pray
has always perplexed me
you're a verbal train wreck
and I listen sometimes to hear what ignorance you'll
spew today
tomorrow
next disaster
mangling the message of God
it seems the older you get the more your personal truths
rattle from your bones
you've always had a problem
discerning fact from fiction truth from lie
testimony from sanctimony

and Pat
Haiti needs your compassion
like they needed Bonaparte
but I wonder what pact have you made
with your devilish God
shame it wasn't to win your freedom from hate

ENOLA GAY

Enola Gay.
Your name sounds like happy.
Like going to the park on a beautiful day
and finding that vendor, the one who sells ice cream
precariously perched on a cone so
you lick around the edges,
secure a foundation, don't want your bounty to lose
its purchase. Don't want it to fall slowly,
hitting the ground, exploding into tastes
you will never taste again
like the first time, like not one cloud
in the sky and soaring through the air.
Your name sounds like foreign places.

Enola Gay.
Your name sounds like a party.
The party no one ever wants to leave.
So we dress in our finery.
We look so fine. We wear hats with flowers
that mushroom bloom off of their sides
and dainty gloves that caress our fingers, taper at wrists.
Pearls harbor our throats like long ago Decembers
and we drink. We drink from shallow cups, pinky fingers
extended, tactical perfection. We talk
about our day, about the future with no regrets.
Your name sounds like forever.

Enola Gay.
Your name also sounds like a question.
So I lean, move in close, and you don't move away.
Hip to hip, phantom fingers trace cheeks
searching for answers. Your smile,
a candle lit, and we watch the smoke tendrils
float toward heaven. You become
your own island and your brilliance, it sparks,
it's radioactive like you could blind us

all with what could be your love.
Your name sounds like a promise.

Enola Gay.
Your name sounds like you were once
somebody's mother. That boy, Paul,
I remember that boy. He wanted to be a fighter pilot
in the United States Army, wanted everyone to know
that you were his mother, so he plastered your name
on an aircraft so they could see you coming.
He wanted you to be the first.
He wanted to make you history.
Then they would know she grew a hero.
He wanted you to see the world,
wanted the world to see you.
First stop Japan, Hiroshima?
Somewhere over there.
You would be at the party.

I imagine when he sat in the cockpit
he mused it was your womb again,
knowing full well foreign seed filled your now-iron belly
as he flew you over foreign places
and when your iron womb gave birth,
expelled your seed, your new little boy,
he fell slow like smoke tendrils
floating toward heaven in reverse. He hit
the ground exploding into tastes
they'll never taste again
like the first time, tactical perfection.
Happy flowers bloom, mushroom cloud,
the only one in the sky. Your brilliance,
it sparked. It was radioactive, a spectacular sight,
it flashed, snatched shadows,
flung them onto concrete walls.
Their dainty hands wore no gloves,
no pearls harbored their throats
like long ago Decembers.
It was a party some would never
leave—like a promise.

And history,
history may remember you differently.
It may not remember that you were once a mother,
raising your own little boy,
his love, his future on your lips like a whisper.
History may not remember you as an actual person
at all, just this thing that could repeat itself.
But Japan, Japan will never forget your name,
because your name,
it sounds like a country,
like a son who loved you so much it killed.

With no regrets.

DELILAH

It didn't have to be this way.
All I wanted was for you to love me
the way I loved you—exclusively.
Just look at me. I am beautiful
and in love with you.
The way I catered,
took care of your needs.
I loved you hard.
Why couldn't you see my love the way
you saw your unseen God?

And what exactly could he do for you that I couldn't?

This is not about trust or faith. This is about us.
I made you first; you made me second thought.
When you opened your eyes in the morning,
I wanted to be the first face you saw,
the last thought on your mind
as you drifted off to sleep.

I never wanted to take your strength.
I just wanted you to love us more
than you loved the other things.
But you kept choosing other things,
then you'd come lay your weary head in my lap
so I could ease your tension.
And I let you.
I let you use my love for camphor.

And I couldn't stop thinking that
if this was the future, your God might not be God.
What if it was women, or money, or power?
And if this was the future
these scissors might not be scissors.
They might just be golf clubs or a cigar
in a room in the White House.

I thought that in order for you to see my love
for what it really was, I needed to cut away those things
that blocked your view—just a little trim.

Remember your Delilah loves you,
and it didn't have to be this way.

GOING ON A BENDER

I consider the boots.

The way they mold to calf and step.
The way they add a little extra swagger to my stride.
When I don the hat,
I tilt it so that it nearly covers my right eye.

The glue applied carefully to my upper lip
will hold the hair cut from my own head.
Maybe I'll wear a goatee today and sideburns.

The corset. The corset will confuse some,
but I don't bend for them, so I don't give a shit.

The way I figure it, if you are talking about me,
if you are judging me then your would-be-bully tongues
aren't lashing someone else's questioning
thin skin black and blue.

There are those who care so much
about what this world thinks of them
they contort their spirits
into people they will grow to hate.

And I don't do that shit no more.

I have grown into my defiance. Long gone are the days
when my response to people who felt it was their job
to point out that
I don't look like a girl!
was to pull down my pants in their presence, check,
make sure my pieces were still there.
I mean if you are going to tell me what I look like
try not be a pussy coward and stomp off
when I report that my vagina is still intact.
What I look like is only relevant to me.

I am not your fucking Barbie Doll.

I am my own fucking Barbie Doll.

I have been known to wear men's suits, dresses, mesh, lace,
ruffles, vinyl, chaps, and a strap-on,

sometimes all at the same time.

And all that means is that I am different on different days
because days are different on different days.

And if you are of the small-minded ilk who believes
that clothing or fingernail polish makes the man or the woman,
maybe you need to come visit my classroom.
But sit your ass in the back! Let the futures I push teach you wha
an open mind looks like and what mind your own damn busines
sounds like.

Today I am going to change the gender in all of my poems.
I am going to bend my poems because they belong to me
like my insane sense of style, my dark, sometimes twisted
sense of humor.

Grateful that my parents had the foresight to know
that this world would try to box me in, lock me down
so they made my skin a key.
So yes, I'm definitely wearing the boots.
But I'll defer to my inner boi scout,
put my strap-on in my bag.

I mean, I have got to be prepared.
Never know what I might need.
I am going on a bender.

TEA PARTY

Those people in glass houses
drink their tea from short porcelain mugs,
Earl Grey with strings attached.
They prefer their tea like their views:
watered down, devoid of flavor.
They have forgotten the gravity of rocks.
Like stale biscuits and old mentalities,
you can't take slave owner out of master.

They like their campaigns
like their country clubs: all white.
I mean, all right, wings
sprout from prosthetic backbones bending truths,
spinning lies like webs of interests
they are not interested in.
Your truths have no place in their house,
the glass so thick nothing can be seen clearly.

Pinky finger arched,
good manners,
crooked ties.
Words disguised as fact,
not meant to be taken as factual,
meant to be taken with cream:
white washed by the new would-be minority.
Fear runs rampant in this house of glass,
this house of mixed messages.

They hold their cups with two hands,
careful not to spill a drop.

DISTRACTED (BABY VEGAS)

My mother insists that we bring them here
once a month—the minimum—more if she has her way.
The atmosphere pleads for my departure.
There are *bings* and *bongs*, screaming children,
a rat sings "Happy Birthday" in the corner.
BABY VEGAS! CHUCK E. CHEESE'S!
Where they purchase gold coins to win tiny pieces
of paper so they can buy their way into a plastic world.

It is stressful here.

Overstimulated, I extricate myself from the bedlam.
I take to the streets, a strip mall. It's the best I can
do in my present environment.
I decide to watch my fellow Americans
do the consumerism thing.
Watch them swipe pieces of plastic so they can
buy their way into a world of debt.

That's when I notice the child, he is two,
maybe two and a half.
He leaves the store without a parent.
He is laughing, playing, having a grand old time.
He hugs the storefront window—fishbowl.
He is playing hide and seek with those who
don't know he's hiding, so they don't look.

My instinct is to grab him up return him to those
who have lost sight of him. Then I remember
I have done this before, and I don't live in that
world any more, that random-act-of-kindness world
where the lost could be returned
without police involvement.

I decide I will watch while I wonder

who else is watching
and is it kindness or nefarious thoughts
in their minds?

Almost ten minutes and this baby is growing daring.
He is exposed to the streets.
I say fuck it, I will reunite this one with the ones
who have no idea where he is
and ease my own conscience.
That's when it happens: his mother flies from the store,
grabs him up, shakes him violently,
scolds him for going missing.
I suppress my urge to shake her, remind her
that she is the watcher, he is her treasure,
but I don't.

Instead I am comforted by the fact that I will not
have to watch a story about this child on the evening news.
Some story about a child
gone missing,
or murdered,
or worse.

People watching is stressful here.

So I return to the foray. I return to the
bings and *bongs*, screaming children, and singing rat,
grateful that my own child is locked down
in Baby Vegas.

Chuck E. Cheese's!

Where a kid can be a kid.

VIVISECTION

viv-i-sec-tion noun
1. the action of cutting into or dissecting a living body.
2. the practice of subjecting living animals to cutting operations esp. in order to advance physiological and pathological knowledge.

1

nostalgia is looking toward the future
while trapped in the past stuck rooted thick
cradled wrapped in old dreams
that were no longer supposed to matter

2

it was always difficult to watch your attempts
to recover your scattered sense of self
fully aware that we were no stranger
to mixed emotions filled with abrupt silences
that reality with us came equipped with habitual
backdoors crooked smiles and partial truths
the way you loved lighting matches
throwing them on my temper feeble attempts
to control what you could never understand

3

it took me a long time to realize how weak you
really were it's the only way I could ever forgive

4

the way your tongue strummed my name
like a fast-forward lie like an instrument you
never intended to learn to play
I clung to premeditated thoughts of failure knowing
this will be no different because I am no different
stuck in this gag reel on demand and you will never
hear me inside your voice over and over and over again

5

no matter how much I stretched my lungs
for your edification my words always fell on deaf ears
I became disgusted by the sight of you engorging
yourself on the foolish notion that you knew everything
about me   how could you   when I never showed
you my face covered the scars I'd have to explain
lined my lips with omissions held another's image
in my heart knowing somewhere in my center
that if I gave you full disclosure I would be excavating
a past you were not worthy to know
you can never know who you never knew
despite the lies you tell yourself in those moments
of many when you alter your mind to match
your skewed perceptions

6

palms up
surrendering to your pretentious charm
me this handy problem solver who believed
you in need of a sympathetic ear always fascinated
by your ability to go from fire and brimstone
to smoke and ash between syllables
no amount of understanding made you clearer
you became a large luminescent lie lingering in hindsight
and I thought I knew better

7

the way your arms hung at your sides
a marionette strings cut I knew
no amount of restringing could raise your self-esteem
your constant disappointment clung like spider webs
shimmering displaying complicated
patterns you knew well reinforced daily
they were holding you together
while tearing you apart watering down an emotional
palette already lacking the colors of conscience

you were too concrete for this abstract mind
I tried to settle for what is because I could never
again have what was

8

I was mindful of the twists and turns the hands
that learned to touch you beyond your voice
trying to smooth your edges hardened
by neglect and abuse
I blamed you for neither though you seemed content
to hold me responsible for both
our immersion into oblivion your spiraling disconnect
misery personified and though I am no mason
I knew my foundation could not hold us both
and I was only prepared to sacrifice in increments

9

I would burn you in effigy if I thought it could cure
thought it could loose you like the tendrils of smoke
escaping our lips habits die hard and traps are traps
whether we set them ourselves or not
it was clear our relationship suffered
acute numerical ascension
meaning our number was up minutes after it started
I wanted simple you said you wanted the same
lesson one ignored like my reflection those alabaster lies
tucked between shoulder blades provided you protection
when your back was against the wall
I remained out of sight
you never noticed my absence

10

you couldn't possibly have expected me to tear down
the fortress built carefully over years to protect
this labyrinthine heart I am watching you scramble
to covet the broken pieces of yourself you left lying
everywhere like detritus strewn from boxcars

riding rails of regret

no one knows me like I do

the pitfalls I've created bread crumbs broadcast
so I'd remember what if felt like to wander
no one person knows all of me
including me
and here I thought you were paying attention
flames are more than you deserve

11

straightjacket freedom never looked good on me
something about the snugness always leaves me disillusioned
you so close I mistook proximity for caring

12

clarity dawns when you find your name twisted around
conspirators' ears embellished so lavishly so pornographic
that nothing about the moment seems familiar
I don't recognize myself every fiber of my being withdraws

13

thirteen is considered bad luck for many
I consider you bad luck for me

14

I've learned to tell only the parts dissected to begin with
believing implied distance will keep me safe
knowing there are thieves among honorable men
the scent of indecision on their breath
when want finds me hungry for contact
flames in my mouth teasing memories in the middle distance
eyes wet with unspent tears
the hero you were reaching for
no longer fills the suit thought indestructible

a stray dog in need of sustenance weakened slack
I cannot save you

15

in retrospect
losing my first love in the wake of my Judas heart
was the equivalent of being in a bottle with no air
I knew I was going to die but morning came
like she always does gentle and unassuming
she found me there my breath still lodged in my throat
ribs aching from the heartache face tear streaked
confidence shook but alive thirty silver pieces
lining down my spine

INCONVENIENT TRUTHS AND LIES

Lie : You are the best thing that's ever happened to me.

Lie : When we met, the first time I laid eyes on you,
I knew we were meant to be.

Truth : The way your eyes slid across my skin
like you never saw me because you never saw me,
you only saw stages and marquees.
My name in an unforgiving light.

Lie : My heart never molded to another's.
Never held pulse to throat. Never held on for dear life,
as you bent me perfect.
It never happened.

Truth : The way you said forever
sounded like a backhanded compliment.

Lie : The way you never doubted as you doubted my fidelity. My
forked poet tongue, my you-are-the-only-one-for-me mentality.

So it is in fact my fault.
My eagerness to meet your needs.
They way I anticipated your desires, and who the fuck
makes reservations any more?
That way I gave you space.
Never crowded you in or out.
Trusted you at your word.
Ignored our shiny brokenness even
as we left parts of us in public places.
Our impressions knifed into narrow minds.

Lie : I'm so glad we never called this love. Never kissed
it on the mouth. Never let the moon catch us bathing
in her rays all sweat and salt.
Our skin never learned each
other's rhythms.

Truth : And the light stayed off the entire time. We both knew that only those truly in love make love with the lights on. So aren't you relieved to know this was not love?

Lie : I am relieved, too.

CARNIVAL

what it was like
before this
was confusing
running through sand
walking on water
misrepresented by our intentions

place me on the back burner
leave me simmering
until I burn
you never wanted this me
you wanted supplicant
I never was good at that

you push and pull me off course
you are an enigma
I am good at solving
but not at revealing you

we know this but insist on this
tug-of-war relationship
I presented myself as myself
and you liked it
until you didn't

it's what we knew would happen
we knew yet pretended we were
not pretending

we do this so well
will do it again and again
merry-go-round lovers
circling each other like vultures
thick like thieves but our bones hold
more meat than we can handle

MASTERPIECE

When we touch for the last time,
I will trick myself into thinking it is a good thing,
relax into the letting, take down
my hair so your fingers can play.
It will feel good because I will not know
it is the last time that I will let you
touch all of my stuff.

You will leave your fingerprints as evidence at the base
of my spine. I will never question your motive.
I will believe a touch as gentle as yours
cannot sting or leave marks
that can only be seen in flashback memories.
I will think we are moving toward a new definition.
Some new name we will call ourselves.

The notion that you will use my skin
as cover to hinge a door you would close
to me, no key offered as payment.
A sign crooked, reading *No This Girl Allowed*.
I will tell myself you always close your eyes
to keep me on your mind.
I will tell myself this until you believe.

Am I in love with you?

A question I keep posing to myself.
When I answer, I suspect I am a liar.

When we touch that last time, I will been present enough
to know what is happening. Maybe I will see
what of me is excavated, what parts are archived,
what pieces of me will be museumed memory.

Then maybe.
Maybe then, I will register the end.
Still I will not be prepared.

THE ART OF OVER PROCESSING

it was beautiful
the way the wind can be beautiful
not seen
but felt
fierce
spinning on the inside

this is what you thought you wanted
then you realized you were thinking
and who goes with the flow when they
are thinking things through so now

we are thinking about it
and we think we are perfect together
we fit like square pegs
punched into round holes
but the fact that we thought about it
lends to amending
then trying to change the other

the perfect we believed we were
before we thought about it so much
has developed a lisp
dragon's breath
burning those things
no longer appealing
because they weren't what we thought
we thought they were
we were whispering
when shouting was in order
covering our answers so the other couldn't see
secretly hoping they'd get it wrong

my voice
would never have made you hesitate
when we were beautiful
when we were perfect

when you touched me in places I rarely showed
when the sound of me
drew you in
didn't cast you away

we are pale edges
involuntary movements
you cannot touch me now
without thinking about it first
you won't allow yourself to sink into me
you are afraid I might think to let you drown

I can't help but think that if we acted more
thought a little less maybe
just maybe
we wouldn't have been
the last thing we fucked up

FOR MY DAUGHTERS

Daughters,
if you should ever meet a man
who promises you the world wrapped in kisses
with lush green gardens, a platinum card
and the keys to all of your dreams,
let him know:

you come wrapped in your own world,
equipped with sensible things like paper, pens,
like the dreams you have achieved so you amended them.
You come with lips made for more than kissing,
the gardens you tend feed your own belly,
and platinum cards often come wrapped in platinum lies.

You are old school because your mother is old school.
That means you are more than willing and able
to put your cash money where your mouth is
and keys just make a lot of noise.

Your dreams will never be locked down.
You will never fully be tethered
to anything but your own destiny.

Daughters,
if you should ever meet a man wrapped in poet tongue
who wants you to believe you are his muse,
writes you pretty poetry, leaves it under your pillow,
metaphors you banquets that won't fill your soul,
holds you accountable for his misgivings,
your words against you,
attempts to restrain your creativity
because he has lost his perspective,
let him know:

your mother is a poet. You are her muse,
her reason for raising the sun each and every morning,
letting the moon loose at night,

and that your pillow is not a paperweight,
it lives in your own house
that you only allow him to visit
when you want him,
and you need more than pretty words to feed your soul,
that the women in our family are fueled by drive
and if his license is suspended
then his ass will be walking.

And if anyone tries to control your creativity,
well, the person who attempts this insane feat
may as well put his head between his legs
and kiss his sorry ass goodbye
because after she,
your mother,
dispenses her own rough justice on him
she'll be back for her daughters
because that is what a mother does.

My beautiful daughters,
I cannot teach you what to look for.
Deception has gotten cleaver
in this age of technology and layered lies
but I can show you what not to lose sight of:
yourself.
Any man who can't love you for who you are
in the moments that you are,
your faults and your divinity,
let him know
that mothers and daughters,
especially this mother and these daughters,
don't fool with such nonsense,
and if his lips move to ask you why,
send his trifling ass to me.
Let him know that
I love you like a combined 23 hours of NATURAL
childbirth and no man is going to love you
like that!

UNLIT

A candle sits by my bedside table
and I want to strike a match,
to kiss the wick, to watch the flicker,
the glow, because to me,
nothing moves as beautifully
as flames dancing.
But unlit it remains.

I have owned it for more than eight years,
earth-toned inspiration waiting to be realized,
waiting for a spark from me,
but it remains unlit.

I have a son, Zion. He is this amazing man-child
who reminds me of, well, me.

He's smart. He's funny.
And okay. He is a little twisted. He got that honestly.
But at the age of four he was conditioned to believe
that a lit candle meant a party, and not just any party,
a birthday party, and no matter the month,
the birthday had to be his,
so in good conscience I couldn't light it.

I'm a mom.
Imagine the guilt if lit and blown out
and when the smoke clears there is no cake.

Even though it remains unlit, it brings me comfort.
Rotund, it sits by my bedside table bearing three wicks,
that fear yet awaits my flame.
Sometimes when my Zion sleeps,
I watch him. He is beautiful
and in my heart I light a wick.
In its glow I can feel it stoke the fires in my belly
and it burns restoration. I light another.

In its illumination
I can see my Zion in the future.
I look forward to those days.
I light the third, and transfixed
by the synchronized movements of flames dancing
to the rhythm of his breathing, I realize
he is perfect, and I want to be just like him
should I ever choose to grow up. I want
to be held in that innocence. I want to be cradled
in that four-year-old logic that says:

Mom, why do I have to take a bath?
You do know I'm just going to get dirty again.

I want to be rocked in the security of knowing
that everyone loves me because that is what love means.
I want him to hold onto that
before this world tries to extinguish his brilliance.

I toss the thought up as a prayer.
It morphs into hope and then a wish.
When I blow out the flames and the smoke clears
for my Zion let there always be cake.

FOR LORRAINE

I'd like to tell you that your wishes were granted
that the foundation you set is stable
and the seeds you broadcast took root
in rich soil and grew tall reaching toward the future
I'd like to tell you all these things
but they would be lies
and lying is an art I've never mastered

if I were a liar
I suppose I could say
that the adventure playground still thrives
that the swimming pool and parking lot
are only figments of our wilting imagination
I could say that the peace garden flourishes
the perennials are bright and bold
and the tiles painted and fired still boast the names
of those who've passed and still shout hopes
for the future set in mortar by tiny hands
and their proud work stands intact
not in pieces

the buildings are not falling apart
collecting wildlife has not become
more important than the human minds
who occupy the buildings
where there was once a waterfall
in the library that flowed for three whole years
that empowerment is still the bread we feed ourselves
and the children daily
we eat heartily
our bellies filled with insight and inspiration

I would tell you that integrity
is still paramount here
that doing what's right
is not considered insubordination
that undermining and too many cooks

in the kitchen is not the reality
that what is needed is always granted
and your ten-year hiatus has not left dreams
destitute and malnourished
because the foundation was set
and the right thing is always the right thing
even though the right thing has not shown its face
recently

I'd tell you that those who remember
still look for you
those who remember
still look out of their windows some days
and see you twirling in the light rain
hands open and raised to the heavens
willing it to wash away and renew
and those who remember
held onto the memories
until they were yanked out from under us
in the form of lies and letters
written by those who never knew you
those who come after this may never know you existed

I would tell you
there was an award once in your honor
I won't tell you that they spelled your name wrong
I won't speak of coroners vans and HAZMAT teams
I won't discuss the disconnect
or the drunken strongholds unsteady on their feet

I will tell you instead
that those you brought into the fold
will remain as long as they can
deflect as much as they can
and hold onto your ideas and philosophies
despite the abridged versions
you can get online
but never in the palm of your hand

I will tell you

that though we were not agreed in all things
we disagreed more often than not
I understood when you remarked that some people
should not work with small children
this is why you didn't work with small children
why you chose those who could put them in place
the main part still rings true
some people should not work with small children

I will tell you
that I know you had no idea you would leave so soon
but if you had put your wishes on paper
willed them to those left behind
maybe I wouldn't have to recount the last ten years
to you with lies and half-truths
that become whole in the retelling

they don't remember you here
there is no room for what worked
but when I leave
and I am being forced to leave so I will go
but I will remember
and take the parts worth preserving

see in order for this new way to work
the old ways have to be removed
democratically
especially those who bark too loud
and bite too hard
I am loud
and my bite leaves marks
and I believe you knew this day would come
I believe you tried to warn me
and the others

we are listening now

I'd like to tell you that
things will be better when we

like you
leave this place we tried to hold onto

I'd like to tell you all these things
but they would be lies
and lying is an art I've never mastered

WHAT LONELY LOOKS LIKE

Leftovers left too long are unrecognizable.
The cheese wears a coat fuzzy and warm
next to the butter that has seen better days.

There are no vegetables. There is no fruit.
The chips are stale. There is no bread.
The cupboards are bare. Nothing here is alive.

If mustard, pickles, and mayonnaise were delicacies
my hunger pains could be ignored.

Ice chills in the freezer, the coolest place in the house.
Something resides in the aluminum foil surrounded by
banked snow. In the future, archeologists may give it a name.

There is water so I drink. I'll pretend it fortifies.
My stomach complains. My hand pats my belly, rubs
in a circular motion. Reassurance that better days are ahead.

NO HOMO

homo - a member of the genus homo
which includes the extinct and extant species
of human beings characterized by superior intellect,
articulate speech, and upright carriage;
also a loanword, a prefix meaning the same

but how can that be

from the moment we are evicted from the womb
we are taught, instructed, threatened
be different
draw your own lines in the sand
create your own existence
be unique, be distinct
be different

because if we were all the same
then our moon would orbit the same earth
and I could stand in the state of North Carolina
Colorado or Georgia with the woman of my dreams
and we could declare our love knowing our rights
would be equally protected because we are the same
but we are not the same, we are different
no superior intellect
no articulate speech
no sense this phrase *no homo*
make no sense to me

well maybe it could, might, make sense
if it erupted from the mouths of my students
who are pissed off and angry
adolescent fists raised in protest
thesauruses, dictionaries strewn about the floor
spines broken, collateral damage
and they are roiling, they are overcooked
alphabet soup letters sloshing off their sides
as they make known their agenda

declaring in loud voices:

WHAT DO YOU MEAN
THERE ARE WORDS THAT SOUND THE SAME
BUT ARE SPELLED DIFFERENTLY
AND HAVE THE AUDACITY TO MEAN
DIFFERENT THINGS!
THEY ARE PRETENDING TO BE SOMETHING
THEY ARE NOT!
WE WILL NO LONGER DEFINE THEM!
WE WILL NO LONGER UTTER THEIR SYLLABLES!
NO HOMONYMS! NO HOMO! NO SAME!

And if it happened like that in a very fucked up
lazy way it could, might, make sense

but when I hear those words in your songs
your poems or your laws
I get the feeling you are declaring your own agenda
expressing your fear of sameness
fear of people who prefer people who look like them
not you, those no heteros
and you are roiling, you are overcooked
alphabet soup letters sloshing off your sides
LGBTQAI

I stop listening
your world is so small and your views are so narrow
they couldn't possible hold someone the likes of me
a member of the genus Homo
of humans beings
characterized
by my superior intelligence
my articulate speech
and this upright carriage

and you are right
we are no homo
we are not the
same

WHAT TO DO WHEN A POLITICIAN TRIES TO FALL INTO YOUR VAGINA FEET FIRST

my body is not yours to pump
lobby or legislate
there are no campaign funds
tucked in my moccasins
or between the folds in my flesh
and the last time I checked
there was no ATM in my vagina
no fuzzy slipper morning sickness episiotomy
no sling back in time mentality
there simply is no room in my womb
for your party to meet
my fallopian tubes are not ear buds
eager to listen to your rhetoric

all you want to do is get in my business
and you have no business being down there
if I wanted you down there
you would have been invited
all shiny and six-inch stiletto
but you were not invited
you just want to barge in
all steel toed and Timberland
so you can cross train tell me
how to run what I have been running
all of my life

what's sad is that I understand your God complex
you've been planting your flag
in other folks' intentions for so long
and some habits die hard
but I'm thinking that if your God
really wanted you in my pants
he would have made you me

I don't have time for your nonsense
the way you flip flop agendas

stumbling on the untied laces of your
misplaced metaphors
confusing women of today
with those you tried to deny the right to vote
with all of your platforms and oversteps

I am sure that you in your supreme wisdom
can understand this discussion is inappropriate
and since you *can't* walk in my shoes
I'm going to need you to take them off
you are scuffing up my shine

but
if you want to discuss fair housing
equal pay for women
educational benefits that ensure
each and every one of my children
goes to college
or if you want to discuss healthcare
or basic human rights
I'd be down for that

but
if all you want to discuss
is how you think I should honor my body
you are wasting your breath
you cannot dictate who lives in my womb
or who is evicted

why would I let you decide when I have a choice
how dare you suggest I get over it
that my body should just shut it down
no matter how many times you say it
there is no such thing as *legitimate* rape

and for the record
women taught the world how to make lemons into lemonade

so until the day
your blood begs for its breath

as you lay broken and battered
some foreigner's seed spilled in your sacred spaces
while those who are supposed to protect
create laws that make you target
     victim
          agenda
               inconsequential
as they abort your dreams
while celebrating your injustice

the day another human being falls
from *your* body like grace
that will be the day you can walk in my shoes
but until then
politician
when you try to get all up in my business uninvited
I'll be shutting that shit down!

WIDE OPEN FOR BUSINESS

when your mouth is full of nails
your heart jagged spikes
and you are neither vampire nor messiah
what are your options

understandably skeptical
you may choose to explore
the coincidental geography splayed before you
divide it
conquer it
or devour it
you may even consider if only for a moment
a brief flirtation knowing you might possibly
go to hell for your thoughts and actions
and since you're going to hell anyway
why wouldn't you expect Lucifer to be hot
wrapped in skin you could explore
and even if your attempts are thwarted
by flames that singe the eyebrows
right off your face you just had to go there
because it was an option
had to try to fit the taste of it along the grooves
of your tongue
some destructions are worth the effort
some truths partner with lies and your halo
needed upgrading a while ago

it's okay
you think to walk tightropes with no safety nets
it's special when your ocean touches shores
not yet claimed or plundered
(you keep a flag in your pocket just for such occasions)
it's beautiful when comets on different trajectories
change their directions crash and form new worlds
this existence has been built on such phenomenon

so
you eat the forbidden fruit
you dive where it is clearly marked
don't do that shit you could die
you touch the third rail
rather go in a blaze of glory no fizz
rather hold the world on your shoulders like Atlas
then for shits and giggles bowl the damn thing
hope for a strike

I once became so accustomed to my own silence
that I held my heart hostage
held my tongue for safe keeping
but safe
is boring
and hostages get released one way or another
the nails beneath my tongue
know where to anchor themselves
and I've been slaying demons
with spikes sharper than
the ones I tucked between my shoulder blades
for decades

I am no martyr or saint
the only blood I hold sacred is my own
coursing through veins
having seen things done things
that would stand your teeth on edge

but in all of this
I have managed to salvage a few things
like my wicked sense of humor
really
who cares if you don't get the joke
I laugh every fucking time I hear it
this sharp wit and a willingness to spar for sport
a warm spot behind a breast plate
scarred from life's harsh realities
but resilient and ready for new possibilities
this kinship I share with pen and parchment

the way they both accept my words without judgment
because they know that truth is arbitrary
and they know
how I like to keep all of my options open
like my mind

ON HOLDING YOUR TONGUE

She thinks she remembers
the way the girl's hands hovered.
She wanted to know the touch of them.
Wanted to feel fingers massaging
her memories back to before
she forgot to pay attention
when she would bite her lips and pretend
it was the girl's kiss.

Morning on the other side of I miss you
is not her happy place.
On those mornings she sleepwalks her way to forgiveness,
gets stuck in regret and barely manages to keep her bones
above quicksand. She checks her pockets.
Finds her tongue.
Attempts to re-anchor it so she can finally speak.
It's a bad fit.
Falls to the floor. She can't remember the last time
beauty made her jaw drop.

The girl with the hovering hands
wore an apprehensive smile.
Mona Lisa, but darker. The girl held secrets
between her thighs
and sometimes when they shared,
she knew everything.

She would float sometimes,
the girl with hovering hands,
hold clouds between her teeth.
She would blow kisses
over her right shoulder.
She thinks she remembers catching
those kisses. Placing them in her pocket
right next to her tongue,
promising to blow them back
to the girl once she figured out

how to disguise blood spatter.

She thinks she remembers why
things failed. The girl with the apprehensive smile
never knew that she cut out her tongue
so she'd never say anything to drive her away.
So the girl, her hands and her smile
mistook silence for disinterest
instead of the adoration it was born to be.
She thinks she remembers trying to speak.
No sound came.

Midnight on the other side of I miss you
is failing moonlight and false memories.
Those nights she roams an empty house
checking the corners for hovering hands.
She collects the dust she finds,
sprinkles it on her open-wound heart
and hopes for concrete. She fumbles
with sewing needles and razor wire,
trying to stitch back her tongue
so she can finally say what she feels,
unafraid of letting the blood show.

She thinks she won't forget this time
because she can't remember
the last time beauty made her jaw drop.

LIKE LIKE

when my girl touches me
the way she touches me

I like it

I tell her

I like that
and I'd like-like more
please

like-like? what's that?
her smile and a question

so I explain to her
as it was explained to me
by my twelve-year-old son
which makes this a fact

there are two kinds of like
there is like and there is like-like
like is, *I like you*
like-like is, *Yeah, I LIKE you*
my son is explaining the phenomenon
of *like* to me because he *like-likes*
this girl at school
he tells me how pretty she is
how they sat together at lunch
and had
a conversation
she is so smart, she is so nice
I like-like her

my heart swells, crashes
partly because he is more
like me than I imagined
mostly because he is more

like me than he knows
because I, too, am a sucker
for a pretty, smart, nice girl
who eats food and has conversations
but I also sweep up the shattered shards of my heart
every time a girl breaks it
my son will have his heart broken a lot
he is just like his mother

and I want to warn him
explain what the hopeless in hopeless romantic
really means, but I don't really believe that shit
I refuse to believe that romance, in love
or *like-like* is hopeless

I love the way his face breaks open
when he talks about sharing ideas
with this girl that he *like-likes*
he way he wants to give her art
I don't care that he uses all of my supplies
he wants to gives her art
he is just like his mother
he gives her art, and he + art
is his heart and she will break it

and when it happens
we will snuggle on the couch, commiserate
and eat comfort food
I will have ice cream
he will eat those Cheetos
that bear no resemblance to any color on the wheel
and we will hold each other up
the way he held me up when heartbreak
just looked like why is my mom so sad

the day he comes home
tells me this girl refused his gift
he will call himself stupid
he will call his hard work, his consideration
his art junk

he will ask me if there was some way
he could have known
that she didn't *like-like* him the way
he *like-liked* her
so I will ask if I can have his heart
his art
I will remind him that I *like-like* him
the way he is just fine
And I will wonder if this will jade him
but before I can get too lost in that thought

he will tell me about the girl
who sits next to him in science
she's pretty mom
I like her
not like-like, just like
and I will think oh, my boy
you will *like-like* her soon
because he is so full of hope

after this explanation
my girl tells me she *likes-likes* me
a giggle on her tongue
yes, I know she is going to break my heart
but I am so full of hope
I am just like my son
so I simply smile back
I tell her I *like-like* her too
and I'd *like-like* more
please

WHY DO I DO THIS

I stop moving. Consider my answer.
I am not one to walk away from hard questions
when asked directly. There was a time when no one asked.
Back then I was sitting in the edge of my existence
waiting for anyone to ask me anything like
Why do I do this?

Once upon a time
I buried myself in nearly three hundred pounds of flesh.
Closed my ears to art, my heart to passion,
settled myself in complacency, an automaton
I walked through my life functional. I rocked my jobs.
The extra pounds gave my children, my students
more to hug. I did my duties. I cooked the meals,
did the homework, read the stories, played Tooth Fairy
and Santa. Then I tucked three parts of me
into bed at night, and in the dark I cried
fetal-position tears. I did this for years.
No one asked. *Why do I do this?*

I take that back.
Once, my father, he asked me a question.
Something innocuous like *How ya doing?*
My response with shrug of shoulder elicited a storm
in the form of words so palatable that today
they still burn the roof of my mouth.

Theresa, why are you doing this?
Your mother and I taught you better than this!
Love who you want to love,
live your goddamn life and stop trying to disappear!
Don't you know I can see you?

This Rasta profit redemption-songed me,
challenged me to take back my life
pick up a pen and write, his final words to me.
And to make sure I understood, a week later

a massive stroke split his brain in three parts.
Fourteen grandchildren lost their foothold
on the universe. Six children lost their focus.
My mother lost her soul mate and for penance
for my deliverance, I was forced goddess in the face
of losing the one man in my life I knew,
I knew without a doubt he loved me.

Theresa, what do we do?

Being the oldest never felt so responsible.

He's not here . . . he wouldn't like . . .
take him off the machines.

Forever changed I am. *Why do I do this?*

Within three months of his passing
I burst from a cocoon half my size
because I stopped letting
one hundred fifty pounds of guilt ride my back.
I took up the company of parchment,
decided I would let my words flow ink
over any who would hear them.
I vowed that I would never again
get caught up in previous investment traps
that are not in my interest.

So I stand on stages, my voice in a mic
to remind myself to never try to disappear again,
because he can see me.
Can you see me?

And that is why I do this.

GRATITUDE

There are so many amazing people in my life. If I thank everyone by name, this list would go on and on, and honestly, my friends, it can't. I want to first thank my children: Imani, Tia, and Zion. Thank you for keeping it together through all of my changes. Mommy coming out and becoming a poet in the same year? I know it was a lot and without your love and support, my sanity would have been lost. Thank you, Alice Lovelace and Charles "Jikki" Riley, for your love and passion for poetry. You were the first poets I ever heard and your being parents made that shit cooler! Thank you, Dr. Wilson, for seeing a teacher inside of me, which forced me to use my words and paved the way for poetry. Thank you, Karen Garrabrant, for introducing me to the amazing that is slam poetry. My heartfelt thanks and gratitude also goes out to Bryan Borland, Kodac Harrison, Jon Goode, Ken J. Martin, Collin Kelley, April Smith, Darnell Fine, the Art Amok Slam Team, Java Monkey Slam Team, Charis Books, the National Poetry Slam Community, Georgia Tech, Tia Williams, Kesi Shaw, Hasan Davis, Shawnta Earwood, Tony Davis, Red Summer, Lakara Foster, Sally Gustin, Inkera Oshun, Scott Woods, everyone I have ever flirted with, and every girl that ever broke my heart!

ABOUT THE POET

Theresa Davis is the mother of three and has been a classroom teacher for over twenty years. She reclaimed her love for poetry after the loss of her father. Since then, she has been a member of the Art Amok Slam Team and has been voted Best of Gay Atlanta in poetry and spoken word by *Creative Loafing, SoVo*, and *Georgia Voice*. She won the title of Women of the World Slam Champion (2011), has been poet in residence as the McEver Chair of Georgia Tech University, was an Emerging Artist Grant Recipient, and was honored by the City of Atlanta with a proclamation making May 22 *Theresa Davis Day*. [www.theresa-davis.com]

ABOUT THE PHOTOGRAPHER

Linda Costa's photographs are light painted portraits—long exposures created in complete darkness using controlled lighting. All the special effects achieved in her images are done in the moment of taking the photograph, using experimental lighting techniques, not computer graphics. She is known for performing light painting at live events. In these performances her work is fueled by the energy the audience shares. She is a native of Rio de Janeiro, Brazil, and credits her tropical roots for her love of people, color, and movement. She lives in Atlanta, Georgia, with her husband and daughter. [www.lindacosta.com]

ABOUT THE PRESS

Founded in 2010, Sibling Rivalry Press is an independent publishing house based in Alexander, Arkansas. Our mission is to develop, promote, and market underground artistic talent—those who don't quite fit into the mainstream. We are proud to be the home to *Assaracus*, the world's only print journal of gay male poetry. Our titles have been honored by the American Library Association through inclusion on its annual "Over the Rainbow" list of recommended LGBT reading and by *Library Journal*, who named *Assaracus* as a best new magazine of 2011. While we champion our LGBTIQ authors and artists, we are an inclusive publishing house and welcome all authors, artists, and readers regardless of sexual orientation or identity. [www.siblingrivalrypress.com]

CPSIA information can be obtained at www.ICGtesting.com
Printed in the USA
LVOW081025030513

332176LV00002B/23/P